personals > missed connections

I Hope You Find Me

The Love Poems of craigslist's Missed Connections

by Alan Feuer

KNOCK KNOCK®
VENICE, CALIFORNIA

CONTENTS

PREFACE

Alan Feuer

Where I live, in New York City, the local transit authority has
for years placed ads on the subway advising riders: "If you
see something, say something." It isn't often that security
officials have insight into poetry, but in this case, I would argue
that they do. All of the poems you're about to read only exist
because someone somewhere—a lusty Brooklynite or a jilted
San Franciscan—saw something then said something. In the
yearning gap between those acts, this poetry was born.

Or perhaps I should say *found* since, after all, each of the works
that follow was taken verbatim from preexisting postings to
the Missed Connections section of craigslist, which is to the
Internet what all those bygone personal ads were to newspapers
and magazines. It was probably a decade ago that I first became
addicted to the things. Early on, I was drawn to their rawness, to
the way they summoned, powerfully and with an almost artless
beauty, all the prismatic colors in love's emotional palette. Here
was ecstasy, infatuation, sexual heat, sexual anxiety, romantic
awkwardness, erotic bravado—not to mention bitterness,

despair, and jealous rage. It was only later that something else occurred to me: Here, also, was a vast and untapped body of poetry, waiting only to be noticed and given a little shape.

A word on shape: not one syllable in this book has been altered from its original form or order. Each of the poems is intact, precisely as its initial author wrote it. My tasks were twofold. They included, firstly, the act of curation, which mostly meant reading thousands of postings from Boston to Seattle; and secondly, once the best candidates had made the final cut, applying ear and eye, which is a fancy way of saying that I treated the unprocessed product by breaking them into lines then into stanzas.

When I started publishing these pieces in the *New York Times* six years ago, they were basically a novelty gag, used to fill space on those embarrassing occasions when a paid ad was pulled last minute by a cold-footed restaurant or an indecisive auto manufacturer. No one took them seriously—least of all, me. But as I kept reading and the poems kept coming, my editors at the paper and I decided something profound was going on.

If you are open to the argument that the greatness of our great American cities derives from their diversity and density, and that these urban qualities conspire to grant us an enthralling anonymity in a heaving human sea of interaction, then maybe you are open to the argument that Missed Connections are something like the Id of the places they emerge from: the craving, aching, aroused, embittered, angry, and invariably collective expression of a crowd of lonely people all jammed together, but unable in the moment to connect.

(reply)

Because that's the thing: seeing something then immediately saying something doesn't lead to a poem; it leads to a pick-up line. It's only when a painful slice of time is introduced between the two—see, silence, say—that the poetry arrives.

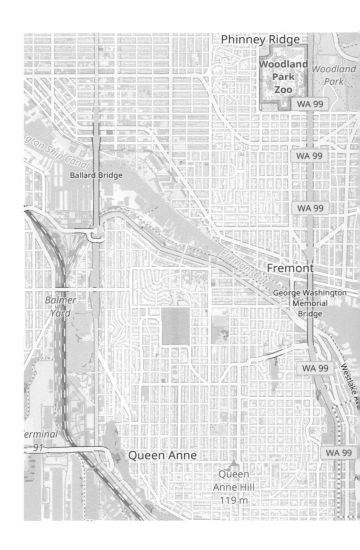

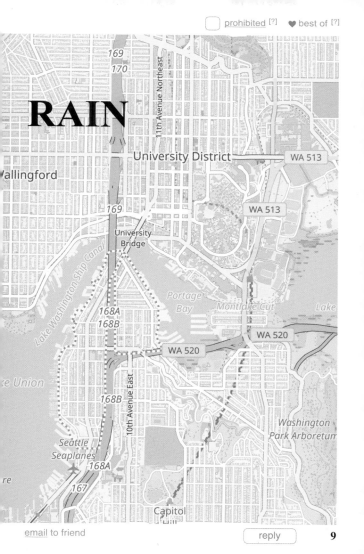

BOLD RED LIP, 100% CHILL IN THE RAIN IN DUPONT

You were walking across Dupont Circle
in the pouring rain today
around 7pm with blond hair,
a bold red lip, and 100% chill.

I was also walking across Dupont Circle
in the pouring rain
with short dark hair, a maroon shirt,
smiling at life
and especially at you.

You smiled back,
with a couple head turns.
Smiling in the rain
is underrated.

IN THE RAIN AFTER A SCREENING OF ANVIL IN E. VILLAGE, I GAVE YOU A CIG

Last wednesday,
in the rain,
at about midnight
beneath an awning
on E. 12th street,
i gave you
a cigarette.

You were walking back east
to meet your friend
who stayed at the concert.
I thought you were smashing
and want to make out with you.

Just saying,
in case you want
to get a drink
(on me) and all...

email to friend   reply

GIRL ON THE TRAIN, GIRL IN THE RAIN

You left work early
but got sidetracked—
maybe that was a good thing.
We got home way too fast for me.
I said this bus ride would last forever,
but it was over in a blink.

You're at Church Avenue
enjoying that cocktail right now,
thinking you should be pouring
two of them.

Your laughter was infectious,
softness under the surface.
You don't know
my neighborhood at all
but want to.

I'm shy—make a move.
Need you to be strong.

TAXI
LIGHTS
IN THE
AUTUMN
RAIN

It had just started pouring down rain
and the city lights streaked second ave.
You were at the corner of 5th street
at the stoplight as I walked up.
You had DVDs in your arms
and, like me, no umbrella

you were gazing at a limo
shouting down towards Houston
and I was looking north for a cab.
Our eyes met.

"I am just watching the limo" you sighed.
"I understand" I replied. And I did.
Because I know what it means to be alone.
I know how it feels to long for companionship,
even brief, and to know
you'll never be the one giggling
in the back of a crass white limo.

And I know how it is
to imagine meeting a stranger
and having it go somewhere.
And I know too well how it is
to get the cab and hop in,
only to realize
I really wanted something else.

I really hope you enjoyed your movies.
As a visitor I know
how it can be in this town.

AFTERNOON SHOWER

Here's to hoping
you made it back
to your car dry
from the rain that fell
almost as soon
as I left the bank.

We only exchanged
a glance and a smile,
but had I been
a minute slower,
it would have been
an umbrella

and hopefully
a conversation.

email to friend   reply

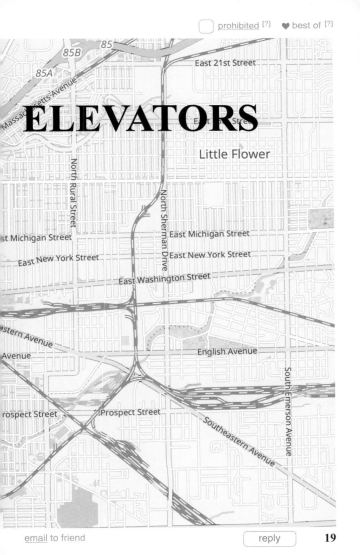

ELEVATORS

Little Flower

CHERRY CREEK, AN ELEVATOR RIDE

You are stuck on replay in my head.
I stared at your bike,
you asked me about the citrus I was holding.
I gave you two sumo mandarin,
without hesitation,
food tastes best when shared.

My floor is the 10th,
why did that elevator
suddenly feel so fast?
As I got off
you gave me your name
and I gave you mine.

I wish I stopped those doors from closing.
I wish I didn't leave in 9 days.
I wish I could see you again.

This is my version of a lotto ticket,
maybe if I'm lucky
you'll email me with our names,
and with your floor number.
I remember which one is yours—
too bad I'm not crazy enough
to go knock on every door.

email to friend

reply

BAY CENTRE BOOTY YESTERDAY

Dear god. It must be contagious,
I creep missed connections
because it's an old habit.
Never thinking I'd ever
post anything here.

You were on the third floor of the bay centre,
black hair, with your friend
who was obviously unhappy.
I was walking out the elevator,
made eye contact for a second,
and bam. That ass is divine,

I was just chilling doing my thing
and now I'm just so damn thirsty.
Nothing's gonna come of this,
but if you somehow read this,
you should know your bum
is just fantastic. Jesus girl.

ELEVATOR CHUCKLES

We have never met until tonight.
Apparently
in our excited to be out of work
elevator ride up to the garage
time stood still for enough time
for us both to make a cracking joke.

Your beauty and kind voice
caught me off guard
as I almost walked out of the elevator
and into the window overlooking the garage.
I jokingly assured I wasn't jumping
out of the window
as I walked back by the elevators doors
still open
as I gazed one last time
at the most beautiful woman
I've tangled in conversation with.

You cracked back a oneliner
that you wanted to jump out of a window
and before it was too late the doors shut.

If you didn't jump, are not taken
and the Creator allows us
to cross paths again
we should grab drinks!

Just a shot in the dark
highly doubt you read this
but it's the only thing
I could think of that may work
if I don't get to cross your path again.

WHERE IS THAT GIRL THAT CALLED ME THE PIZZA GUY AT LENOX TOWERS?

2014 summer it was
a Friday in May.
I came out of the elevator
of Lenox Towers
and saw two girls
a really pretty brunette
and a blonde who was her friend.

They were both wearing skirts.
And the brunette girl said to me
"are you the pizza guy?"
I said no. And then she said
would you like to get some pizza
and I got really shy and kept walking.

I actually came back
to the same place 5 minutes later
but they were gone.
I just feel really stupid now,
because I feel
like I am in love with that girl
and I don't even know her.

I acted very stupid
and wish I had another chance
to talk to her
and take her out on a nice date
to get to know her.

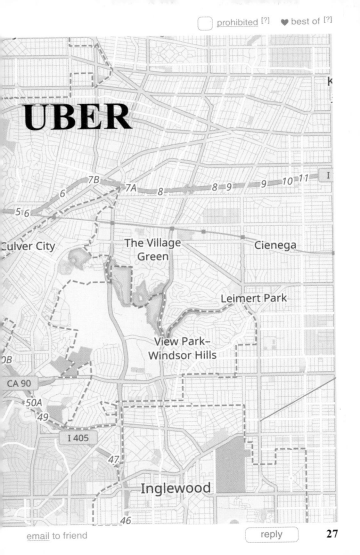

UBER

UBER RIDE TO SFO

I was sleep-deprived and tired
and my head turns to mush
when I try to make a rational point.
I swear I wasn't inebriated or high
and I'm usually not one to indulge in such.

I do wish I took you up
on that offer to drive me.
This weekend could've
turned out differently, like
those ironic indies
that seem to dominate
my Netflix playlist.

email to friend   reply

UBER DRIVER/ARTISTE

We spent the night drinking wine
and watching Ghostly Encounters
and then we had
a couple of sexual encounters of our own
which ended because
we were a little less prepared.

You drive an Uber and you
told me how you used to take
your nephew to school
(despite not being a morning person)!
And you explained the meaning
of your T tattoo...
I lost your number;
please reach out
if you still have mine!

YOU WERE IN MY UBER POOL
SATURDAY NIGHT/SUNDAY MORNING

I am a white guy
with sorta long brown hair
(to my shoulders).
You are a white woman
with black hair and a nose ring
of some kind.

You were wearing a striped shirt
and I was wearing a t-shirt with a pocket.
We got in the same Uber Pool
on Sunday around 4 am.

We were both in North Brooklyn
or whatever you want to call it
—I got in the cab near North 6th and Driggs.
Don't remember where you got on,
but you were really beautiful.

You talked about the bar you came from
playing Slayer and Pantera,
as well as us both enjoying Mexican
and Vietnamese food.
You showed me your tattoo of a naked lady
on your right arm.
We seemed to share the same dread
for having to go to random shit
to support our friends, like
you going to your friend's art show the next day
and me going to North Brooklyn
for my friend's birthday.

I also mentioned that I was baked
and you seemed to share my love for weed.
The sun was rising and you said
this was what every day of summer was like.
Anyway, you got off in Sunset Park somewhere
and before you left you looked at me,
and in that moment
I knew I fucked up
by not saying anything.

UBER LOVE

we took uber pool together from oakland
and we dropped you off in emeryville,
as i was on my way to berkeley.

we discussed great things
including fungus
(I said a silly rhyme, film, music,
sleeping on a porch,
and a future limo business idea.)

when you left,
the uber driver said we hit it off
and should have exchanged digits.
anyways i miss you already
lets fall in love
and tell each other secrets.

reply

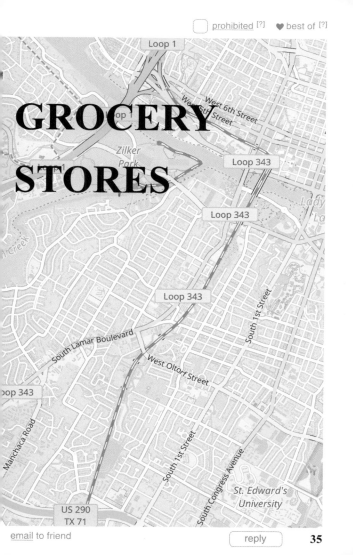

GROCERY STORES

TRADER JOE'S MONDAY EVE.

You = a reading dancer
(modern) of art.
I, a cashier reader
(modern) of comedy.

Hoped you noticed
I treated you extra nice =
The Golden Rule for cashiers
with a customer crush.

So much to forget,
so much to remember—
what Swan Lake did we speak?

I type these words
because I believe in fate—
if you read them on
the world wide web
does that mean anything
or just a thing?

Returning a lost wallet to the owner?
Contents intact. Missing or,
catching the Train just in time?
To feel at ease with someone
that you find intimidatingly beautiful—

the hands that usually shake
move smooth and languid
in a small vocabulary.
What would Miro say?

DAIRY INDECISION

OR

MOOCHING AIR CONDITIONING

You and your baseball cap
were either in dire crisis
about what dairy products to get
or you were just milking—
no pun intended—
the freezing cold air for all it was worth.

I would've asked you directly,
but you were on the phone.
This would have been 15 minutes
or so before the 9:45pm showing
of *Inglourious Basterds*,
which is why I didn't dilly-dally
to see if your call would ever end
and open a window for conversation.

Anyway, hit me up.
I swear I don't say
"dilly-dally"
in real life.

6TH/LAMAR WHOLE FOODS, 3 YEARS AGO

you were a cashier.
i'd engineer my place in line
so i'd show up at your register.
you were tall, thin, poised
and beautiful—
had a confident air about you.

then you were going to school.
and then it was sxsw
and you told me you used
do 512 to find free shows.
it seems like i'd always just left the gym,
so had a meal from the hotbar
or the cafe.

you noticed I had chocolate milk
and said that chocolate milk
was "so much better than whey"
for a post-workout recovery.
You said it twice, exactly the same,
at a couple different times—
I thought it was cute.

I shouldn't remember you.
maybe you will fade now.

KNOW WHAT I LOVED MORE
THAN GROCERY SHOPPING

Laundry. Your clothes.
dancing with mine,
entangled, wet and chaotic...
How would that be?
I wonder...

Maybe it would be sort of like
waking up next to you
more than once or twice or week.
Or like shopping together
for the things we were going to
cook each other.

You wouldn't even eat my spaghetti...
And yet with another line,
they break me to pieces.
I hate you for it, liar.
You love him now,
keep your mouth shut
and go be with him.

TRADER JOE SOLITAIRE

As you seem to be
a talented virtual card player,
I would like to request
a lesson in gaming.
Maybe there are some
card games for two
that might well be played
in a park of some sort?

Plus, I have so many questions to ask you
such as
what the Scottish terrier pin you wear represents
and how you cook your Brussels sprouts.

On the off chance you read my shot
into the darkness,
do respond.

ernail to friend   reply

I WISH...AT WHOLE FOODS

I bet you don't live here...
never ever,
but when I was at the salad bar
putting it in a box at
Whole Foods, Union Square
this evening,
you spoke to me in Japanese

"it's kukiwakame, right?"
You must have recognized
I am Japanese.

You were so beautiful
with white summer cotton dress
and your grey hair
was neatly taken care.
And your smile!
with wrinkles and natural makeup
was just gorgeous.
I was so tired from work
that I gave you only several words.

I wish I could talk with you more
and expressed my impression to you...
I'd like to grow old elegantly
like you.

KEY FOOD MARKET SUNDAY NIGHT

to the cute girl who reached for some hagen daaz
as my man and i argued over the merits of
traditional vanilla vs creme brulee
or dulce de leche ice cream
for our a la mode pie...
he thought you recognized me from somewhere,
i thought you might be interested in us both.
prove me right?

we caught eyes again
as you were in the check out aisle
and we went to the automated checkout.
did i say you were cute?

reply

ZABAR'S

To the guy who crossed Broadway
just behind me, and followed me into Zabar's—
upstairs to kitchenwares—
and browsed while I looked for
and then bought
what I needed;
you left without buying a thing:

You conjured up a ghost—
a memory of a boy I made out
and rolled around with
for several mid-night hours
one night on a mountain-top
in Vermont, in 1991 (I think).

Someone I hadn't met before that night,
and someone I haven't seen or heard from since.
I remember almost nothing about him.
He's not important; I don't care.
But it's nice sometimes
to be forced to remember—

rolling around on mountaintops—
grass stains—accumulating dew.

To the real BG,
I wish you the best.
And to the guy at Zabar's,
I wish you the best.

YOU FARTED
IN WALMART

You were the tall brunette
with the near perfect body
that farted
in the bread section last night.

I was the tall guy next to you
that looked over and asked,
"Was that you?"
You quickly replied
"No...Wasn't me!"

You almost seemed insulted I would ask.
As the stink grew
you continued to deny your flatulence,
but it was evident.

I tried to get rid of the stench
by waving 2 loafs of Ciabatta bread.
You proceeded to storm off
in an angry manner.

You are beautiful
even if you are a liar
and fart like a Clydesdale,
I'd love to meet up sometime.

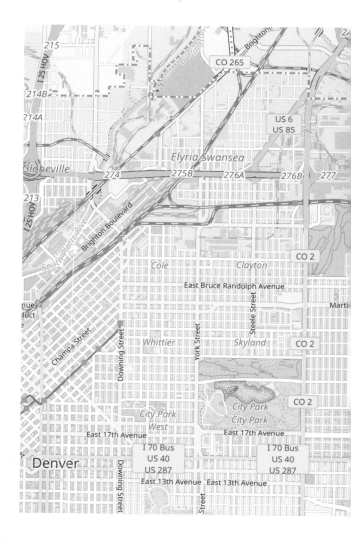

prohibited [?]   ♥ best of [?]

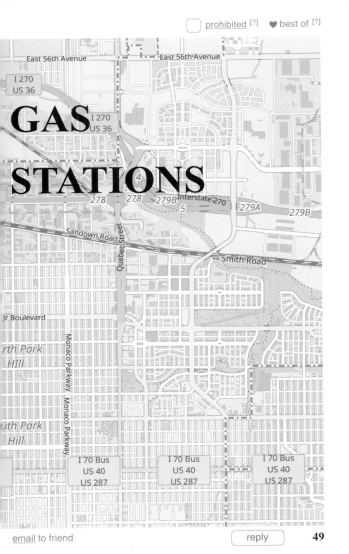

GAS STATIONS

MODELING UNDERWEAR OUTSIDE
GAS STATION AT LAMPLIGHT

I saw you in your car
as I walked out of the gas station.
By the time I got over to my truck
you were out of your car
in your underwear
digging through the trunk and back seat.

You got back in the front seat,
then got back out and did the same thing
in a new pair of underwear lol.
Gorgeous booty.
I was in my company's Ford
at the pump
in a grey shirt and kakis.
Loved the second pair haha

email to friend   reply

I SAW YOU AT THE GAS STATION

I was the brunette pumping gas wearing cutoffs.
My pump went off too quick
& made a real stinky mess.
I guess you're pretty familiar
with that kind of situation
so you just watched me try
to wrangle the flaccid tube.

You were driving a big truck
& playing your music so loud
that my cries for help were drowned out.
I guess during the commotion
a spark was generated.
Not the one between us but
I can see why you would think that,
you big hunk.

No, I'm talking about a real
static electricity induced spark.
It ignited my gasoline moist short shorts,
like the tension between us might have.

But you were already on your way
bumping Florida
louder than my screams would carry.
Long post short, I'm a ghost,
a sexy one at that
but I'm so lonely.
Come play with me.

GAS STATION GUY

You just seem so kind.
And your face is just so nice.
I bet
we would make good friends
cause I bet
you are super cool,
just like me.

GAS STATION OFF NASA

you were a random person
that walked past me
while I was in line
at the gas station

and yelled at me
i was beautiful
it was so busy
I was so shy
and you made sure
that I knew
you were talking to me!

just wanted you to know
you made my day!
and thanks so much
it meant the world
coming from a random stranger

prohibited [?]　♥ best of [?]

ART

CHINESE CONCERT, MOMA,
TURQUOISE SCARF ON HEAD

You were there with your mom
at the Chinese concert at MoMA
in the garden this Thursday.

You had a quasi-rockabilly look to you
—a turquoise scarf wrapped around your hair,
extra red lipstick—
and wrote into your pad here and there,
looked at the Giacometti statue a few times.

We may have exchanged glances.
This, a haphazard throw into the ocean...
but a nice sentiment nonetheless.
You are beautiful
on the outside.

email to friend

reply

THE TITIAN HAIRED GIRL WHO BRUSHES
HER TEETH AFTER SMOKING CIGARETTES

I hope you started your painting.
I hope you began your photo essay.
I hope you're not spending your nights
trying to find clever means
of getting your hands on Xanax.

I hope you're not living
out in the Alaskan wilderness.
I hope you're hurting a little less.

YOU WORK
AT THE
GUGGENHEIM

in the Kandinsky wing, you caught my eye,
i thought you were cute, and wondered how
you came to work at the Guggenheim.
later, i noticed your awesome outfit:
instead of a suit,
a black one-piece coverall-type operation,
with a tie and lots of pins/buttons.

i wanted to talk to you,
but i was too shy!
fat chance you'll see this, but if so,
let's have a drink :o)

i was wearing
a deep plum dress,
with lavender hair to match.

reply   **59**

MOMA PS1 LONG ISLAND CITY

You were dancing close to the steps.
I was standing on the steps
wearing a blue jersey, smoking a cigarette
and drinking coffee (of all things).

You were (and probably still are)
a brunette with long hair, big eyes,
and you were wearing some sort
of a white/pink flowery(?) top.

Our eyes met several times,
smiles were exchanged,
but I never got the chance to say hi to you.
It was my mistake. Hoping to rectify that.

email to friend

reply

RUSSIAN DIVA IN THE ANDERSON COLLECTION

You the tall, blonde Russian
(is there any other type?)
walking through the art collection.
A guy with a weird necklace
and I approached you.

Then we shared a moment
in front of a $50MM Jackson Pollock.
We laughed (whispers,
we were in an art museum)
about NASA wasting hard-earned wages
on a space pen,
while the Russians just used a pencil.

Your quick wit and astute
art observations threw me off.
We made an awkward exit
before realizing our mistake
and running back. But alas!
You were gone

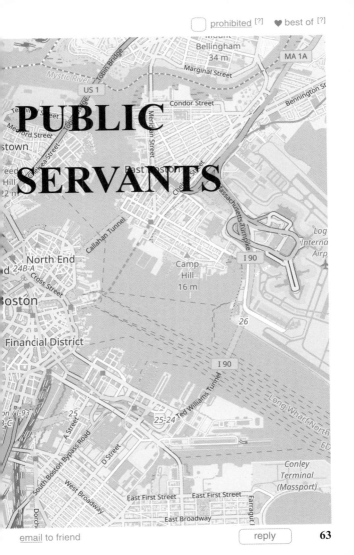

PUBLIC
SERVANTS

IN THE BACK OF YOUR COP CAR SUNDAY

I was detained
in the back of your car
Sunday afternoon.

You were very nice
and listened
to my crazy story.

I liked
being punished.

email to friend

reply

I WAS THE GUY IN THE DOT TRUCK

You went into burger king
and then I seen you run
after two girls
and you had some words with them
and you came back
to stand in front of burger king

and looked at each other
and you told what had happened
and then you said
you were waiting for a friend

and then she came
and you waved bye bye.
long story short
you were very cute

I should have
came over to you
and gave you my #
you were wearing a light blue shirt
and blue jeans.

I was that bald guy
in the orange shirt.

DYLAN, FIREFIGHTER FROM WEST ISLIP, WHERE ARE YOU???

Dylan and I met in Penn station
Sunday at 5:45pm.
I had just missed my train
and Dylan approached me
and started talking to me.

Then he took me to Trax for a drink.
I was actually happy that I missed my train
because I got to spend an hour with him.

Dylan, I was so annoyed
that you couldn't remember my name
that I had to walk away.
But then I decided, who cares?
We're both completely sauced.
So I went back!!!! But you were gone.

Maybe someone will see this
and you can contact me.
So Dylan,
the runner, firefighter from West Islip,
with your cute curly hair,
I hope you find me.

email to friend   reply

SEXY BALD COP

Damn.....last night around 1,
i saw this sexy cop.
He was bald(ing)
and looked like
he was wearing glasses...

i think he works
in the hylan blvd station house
(i saw him on the blvd in new dorp)
he was the driver, i live near by.
maybe we can hookup?

i'm divorced and i really dont care
about your status. Waiting
patiently ;)

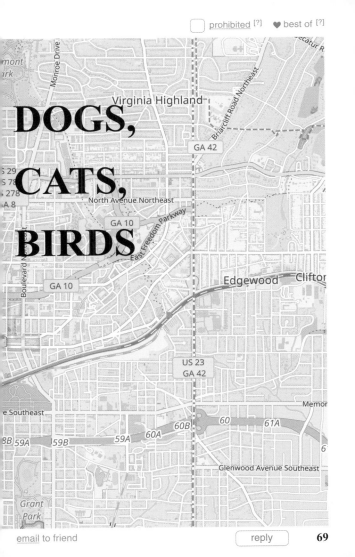

DOGS,

CATS,

BIRDS

BIRD
HANDLER
ON
W 50TH

Wanted to say 'thanks'
for taking your time this morning
to care for the dazed
and confused bird
that was grounded on the sidewalk.

I was glad to see someone
actually care about the poor thing,
especially after the dismissive
building guard started talking.

It generally takes one person
to pay attention to a small beautiful thing
for others to slow down enough to look,
much less help. You did that,
and it was a nice way to start the day.

And thanks to Google
it does look like the guy
who said "Curlew" is right.
Which meant not only
did I experience a rare, clear moment
of nature-meets-city
before heading in to the office,
I also found out where the name
of an obscure NYC experimental band
came from
(my only real Curlew reference before this morning).
Thanks for that.

GREENBELT GODDESS

It was around 5pm on Thursday (today).
The trail was overgrown
with these tall yellow flowers.
I was hiking along the river,
pushing through the brush
across from these limestone cliffs.
I heard a woman laugh
as a dog jumped into the water after a ball.
Then I saw you.

It was hard to look away.
Your skin, this beautiful light mocha color—
you were wearing a white bikini.
I was mesmerized.
You were basking in the sun
on a rock in the middle of the water.

The trail ended close by,
so I lay down in the sun for a while
and watched the dogs play.
On my way home I saw you again
further down the trail.
You were again looking heavenly
on a boulder in the sun with your dog.

We looked at each other
for what felt like an instant and an age.
"I don't want to disturb her moment,"
I thought to myself
and distractedly kept walking.
But I was too caught off guard
by how beautiful you were
that I didn't realize I wasn't actually on the trail.

As I debated going back to talk to you
or not, I realized I was far off the trail.
At that moment your dog bounded right up to me.
He stopped, looked at me,
and then turned around
to go running after you.
"That's got to be a sign from the universe,"
I thought, and I turned around to look for you.
But your dog was too fast,
and by the time I found the trail again,
you were gone.

YOU LOOKED LIKE A DOG

you looked like my dog
I had when I was a child.
she died when I was 3.
I believe you are she,
now in human form.

you were on eckford and norman.
maybe 29 y.o.
wearing a black bandanna.
you looked like you
were on your way back from a run.
and you were hungry...

reply

HOT MAN WITH CUTE DOG

it's not hot or cool
to yank your dog roughly.
dogs are living creatures,
not accessories.

if you're cranky,
breathe in through your nose.
hold it for a few seconds
and then breathe out
through your mouth.

do it with me now.
iiiiinnnnn.
hoooooooooold it.
a little longer.
now ooouuuuuttt.
feel better?

now let your dog piss
on the hydrant
and smell the garbage
thoroughly.

and have a nice day
you fucking meanie.

MONTECITO PET STORE, MESA SHOPPING CENTER, LAST FRIDAY

Or was it Saturday?
Weekend event
in front of Montecito Pet Store,
around 2:00.

You introduced me to
a cute, lazy little grey kitty,
only a little over a year old,
but already a mother cat herself :)

I know you were paid to be there,
talk to the public,
and showcase the cat,
but you were quite friendly.

I would have talked more,
but was very self conscious
about my hair that afternoon....
bad hair day ;)

I'm interested in going to one or more
of the upcoming Campbell Hall
screenings of Bogart / Bacall movies,
would love some company, no funny business.

If you see this and would consider going,
tell me the name of that kitty kat,
and I'll know
you are no random so-and-so.

BIRDMAN AT MATCHLESS

You helped save a bird
from a not so promising fate
by climbing on top of a wall
and safely returning it to it's mother.

Thus you were renamed "Birdman"
and will forever have
a soft spot in my heart.

Would like to discuss in further detail
your future aspirations as a "Bird Rescuer"

in the Brooklyn area.

email to friend   reply

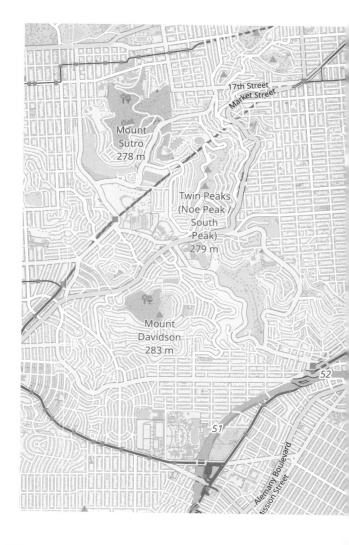

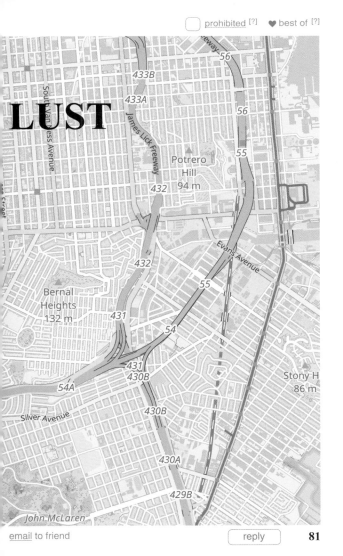

LUST

YOU WORE IT UP AGAIN

I am struck dumb by this attraction.
Your eyes (voice, scent, curves, whatever)
make me so weak,
I just need to lay down for a minute.

I usually can't shut up,
but I see you and I have nothing to say;
I'm afraid I'll keep talking
and never stop.

Please wear your hair down again—
when I see your neck,
I can't get any work done.

With your hair down,
you're merely breathtaking.
I can handle asphyxiation,
but I'm so afraid
I'll touch you on your neck
without permission one day,
and I will have to endure
the shame of becoming
the creepy,
older man,
semi-stalker
pariah

The hopelessness
of ever getting near you
makes me angry at god.

I write here
because
I can never approach you
there

I AM SEEKING TWO LOVELY LADIES

you plucked my heart of strings
and lanyard
you two red headed heartbeats of wonder,
though only one of you has red hair...

the other one...
brown...
brown bunny furr.
fuzzy brown bunny.

email to friend

reply

MUSIC MOVED THROUGH YOU AT BEMBE

You danced.
By god did
you dance.

You wore a turquoise dress-top
over black tights.
When you let down your hair
and shook your head to the music,
I felt like I was watching something
so vital, feminine, sensuous, wild,
and triumphant—
a perfect expression of a woman—
I was captivated.

I could not dance
with you and your friend.
My guests, sardonic designers,
could not set aside their irony
to enjoy dancing.
It was heartbreaking
and ruined my evening.
But you, please, never
stop dancing.

PETITE BRUNETTE WITH THE CUTE PAINTED TOES

OMG.....When I Looked Down
At Your Magnificent Feet,
As You Were talking With Your Friend
In Front Of the Movie Theater
This Afternoon Around 3:30....
Girl.....I Would Luv To have Those
"Cute Painted { Hot Pink Bubble Gum } Toes".....
In My Presence
Every Two Weeks

Or So......that's All.......just To Worship
Your "Cute PAinted Toes"..........
On Your Sweet Beautiful Feet......
Nice Glasses Too........
Fashionable White Blouse Over Denim Shorts.......

Sorry, I'm Not a Flip Flop Guy........
But, I Did Notice
Your Perfect Painted Toes..........?

CIRCUS TALES

Why is it
that every time we get together
the two things we always do
is argue and have sex.

Like the time we went to the circus.
We both argued about going
because we're both animal rights activists
but we went anyway.

I've got to admit we had a pretty
good time and looked kinda cute
in our matching
Ringling Brothers Barnum and Bailey
circus tee shirts.

We waked home along the river
eating our leftover popcorn
and cotton candy.
Your powder blue circus tee contrasted
nicely with the pink cotton candy
so I took a photo with my iphone
that we both posted on our face book pages.

It was actually really nice
lingering on your bed
and watching the sun set.
You told me that the lions
made you feel frisky.
We made love like animals.
Good hard, wet, soft, firm, tender love.

On my way back from the kitchen
carrying a glass of fresh pomegranate juice
I slipped on that old worn out antique rug,
the one you love.
The one I always said was a dust trap.
I spilled the juice all over
your duvet cover. Again
the one I hate but you loved.

You told me how much
you loved that duvet cover,
now stained with pomegranate juice forever.
I told you I thought the splotch of color
was actually an improvement.
That's when you threw
a flurry of nasty curse words my way
and told me to leave.

I know it's only been a day,
but I miss you already.

PORT O POTTY GAL

Amidst the hipster-friendly
sounds of Band of Horses
on a balmy summer night
set against the Manhattan skyline,
we emerged from
the port o pottys
after several tasty Brooklyn lagers.

Soaping up our hands
at the makeshift washstations,
you were aghast to discover
the foot-pump water dispenser
was indeed empty.

After suggesting soapy high-fives,
I macgvyverishly offered
to wash your hands off with my beer,
leaving them clean and hop-scented
as god intended.

After the successful ablutions
as we began to walk back to the crowd,
you disappeared
while I dreamily pictured
our evenings together:

Dinner, at my place...
the scent of exotic spices
dances with your
daintily shaped nostrils,
while you enjoy a handmade cocktail
of your choosing.

We get caught up in the moment
and alas! The food is burned!
No matter, we walk to the corner market
and pick up some beef jerky
and a quart of coffee ice cream.

After dinner, we roll a joint
and have 3 hours of
physical, energetic, reciprocal unprotected sex
(I am clean
and you would be on the pill,
but not that scary one
where you only get a period
once every like 10 years.)

We shape our own reality—
this could be yours.
Godspeed.

GENTLEMAN SEEKS SAVAGE

Ladies of New York: I'll be honest:
my life is getting boring.
I work full time,
and go to law school in the evenings.
In short, I would like
an ill-tempered, poorly behaved
young lady to share some time with.

You should be a complete savage.
A genuine godless heathen
who exhibits at least some
of the following traits:

• Chain smoke (no menthols please).

• Ceaselessly quaff hard liquor
straight from the bottle
after using a black marker
to remove the Surgeon Generals warning;
refer to the time
you "made C. Evrett Koop your bitch".

• Be willing to hurl aforementioned liquor bottle
across the room at me
when I say something you don't like.

• Be willing to work tirelessly
to make my family hate you,
and alienate my friends

• Penchant for self mutilation.

• Touches me inappropriately in public,
in full view of strangers,
co-workers,
family,
and stray cats.

• You do not smell good.
Please note that this does not mean
you smell bad either,
you just can't smell good.
You should bathe in baking soda
to neutralize odors,
and not wear any perfume cologne, etc.
It would be really nice if you smell like
a whiskey soaked ashtray,
instead of smelling like flowers.

• You should be unemployable,
which is very different from unemployed.
You should be irresponsible,
untrustworthy,
and prone to thievery.

• Refusal to eat any food that
has not previously been fried,
or purchased from a vending machine.

• Be willing to violently disagree with everything I say.

• And finally,
you should have tattoos
and piercings,
at least one of which is someplace
you can't publicly display,
outside of the Burning Man Festival,
without fear of being arrested for indecency.

Please respond
if you'd like
to be my savage.

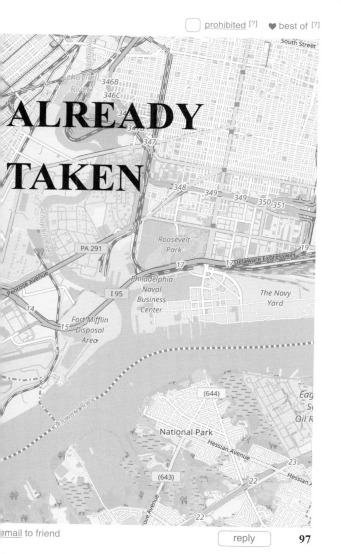

ALREADY
TAKEN

BEATS AND BEAUTY

I was walking into Friends the other night.
I sat down at the bar
and I ordered a Mind Eraser.
Then I glanced at the dance floor.
And, there you were.

You were a tall, shiny long-haired
stunning brunette with cosmic, hypnotizing
light-brown radiant eyes
that lightened up the dance floor.
Your perfect curvaceous and hour-glass figure
with succulent, bodacious big breasts (40 DD)
complemented the dance floor.

You reminded me of Kendall Jenner
but with a more enhanced body. Wow!
And, the way your curvaceous figure
moved in sync with the magical beats
and rhythms of the dance music
as every part of your body
swerved and curved
unlike some without full body control.
I couldn't keep my eyes off of you
as the majestic splendor of your outright presence
grabbed my attention.

I purposely moved closer to the dance floor
to get a better glance,
but I saw you with a big group of friends.
Is any of them your boyfriend?
I hope not. Tell me what song was playing
so I know it's you.

YELLOW COAT AT ZAYTOONS

We were sitting next to you
watching those people
have sex in the window across the street

I thought you were ridiculously cute
and your boyfriend's jokes weren't funny
You seemed bored and kept glancing over

I'm the non-brit
Hoping the other guy
was your brother...

reply

YOU TOLD ME YOU LIKED MY CHEST

You came up to me
and said you liked my chest
unfortunately
my wife got in between us,

I thought you were really cute
and I'd love to let you feel it
uninterrupted
next time

YOU WORE A DARTH VADER SHIRT AND I BROUGHT THE DEATH STAR

It seemed like a match made
in a John Cusack film.
We talked for like an hour about Star Wars,
Monty Python, Laserdiscs, NYC in the 70s
and Midnight in Paris
(and I got a little sidetracked
and never finished my story
about seeing it while in summer exile in Austin),
and I felt a spark.

You waited until that point
to mention your boyfriend,
totally disregarding the 11-second rule.
I really thought you were awesome
until that moment,
but we were both drunk,
so who knows?

So now I have to forget about you,
so I'm writing this message in a bottle
and dropping it into the sea
of the internet.

TO THE GIRL IN THE TREES

We go to the same trucking school...
im struggling to figure out life
and where i want to be....
you're a real man's woman.
too much for me to handle
at least for right now at my younger age (25)
although im fairly sure
you are a year or two younger than me.

you have the most perfect grey eyes
and freckles that accent your bright and
playful almost boyish smile...
you are tall and wispy,
a trait which betrays to sight
your physical strength and resilience...

you have accomplished a lot
more than most women even today
usually ever do and yet
you battle confidence on the field.

You are The perfect woman
for a more mature and aged version of me.
You have a boyfriend and a bright fun life.
I have no chance
and the possibility that someone such as yourself
would be up on this random chance roulette
is slim to nil...i am losing
My hair a bit and wear thin frame
german style round glasses...
my quiet and somewhat awkward nature
hides behind it a mind
full of knowledge and eagerness to know people.....

if you know who i am
reply with the color of my mechanics worksuit.....
then idk what happens from here...
just write me back through the email on here
if u can figure out how....
tell me how weird i am....
wouldnt be the first time...

otherwise goodluck
with all the fun things life has to offer you
and for Christs sake
try not to fall off the crane boom
when your cutting those trees
you adventurer you

BIG
CUDDLY
GUY THAT
KEPT
TOUCHING
MY LEG

You sat next to me
and kept touching my leg.
I told you I was going to see my boyfriend
but you couldn't take a hint.

You just kept talking and touching,
that's when I noticed your friends.
They are both very cute and funny
I was hoping you could get me in touch with them.

You smelled like potato chips,
but they were awesome
and I'd love to see them again.

Maybe you could pay for my ticket
to come see them
as you said you're a millionaire?

WE WERE A PRETEND COUPLE FOR A NIGHT

Just after I had just introduced myself to you,
a drunk acquaintance came across,
asking how long we'd been together,
thinking that we were a couple.
Without missing a beat, you replied,
"Three years," and smiled at me
as though I was truly the man
you had loved for the past three years.

I loved how you played along in that moment
and continued to play along for the rest of the night.
We walked hand in hand in the cold.
Partied at the after-party.
Talked about everything and nothing.
Drank each other's drinks.
Laughed at each other's silliness.
Danced in each other's arms.
Walked together to the train.
Kissed kissed kissed in the cold.
And then you disappeared through the train doors...

I cannot forget how your eyes glitter.
I wanted to take you home that night.
I can still taste your lips.
I want to know if it can be more than pretend.

I hear your laugh in my ear.
I want to make love to you.
I feel your breath against my neck.
I think of you much more than one should think
of a pretend girlfriend.

reply

YOU WERE PUKING ALL OVER THE SUBWAY

Last week
I was taking the D train to Rockefeller Center
to wait all night for SNL tickets.
I was prepared with a blanket, gloves,
hand warmers
and all the other necessities to keep myself warm
while I waited on the sidewalk
for 6 hours.

I was alone on the train
until you and your shitfaced friends came on.
You had to lay down on the raunchy seats,
otherwise you'd feel like
you were in a tilt-a-whirl.

Time passed and you all
were still drunk
and being stupid,
then the rocking of the train intensified...
and the pukefest began.

All of you started one by one,
puking on different areas
of the floor of the train.
I had to tuck my feet in the chair with me
because your colorful vomit
was sliding and spreading
across the floor like hot butter.

I took my things out of my large bag
and handed it to you
so you could finish in it.
You amazed me with your ability to keep going.

The bottom of the bag ended up falling through
and my effort was pointless.
I ended up leaving a glove in that bag,
but it was already wasted.

You finally stopped
and I had to breathe through my mouth
the rest of the time on the train
so I wouldn't puke.
Once my stop came,
I had to make an olympian jump off the train
to avoid your vomit.

I just wanted to say
YOU'RE WELCOME
for lending you the bag
and giving you listerine breath strips
since you never managed
to say THANK YOU.

And don't worry
about replacing my glove,
my hand is still thawing out
from freezing all night.

MAN WITH TATTOO OF HIS AUNT'S SIGNATURE

you: drunk. beautiful
tattoo of your aunt's signature
on your forearm.
overall, a total babe. and
knew something about painting.

me: just got off work.
sweaty, and blabbering.
if it is you, and you would want
to get a drink sometime,
tell me what i was wearing.
and what my tattoo was.
and my favourite book, and color.
(last two not required)

BLACKED OUT IN YOUR APARTMENT

Hey Dudes! I'm hoping
this finds the two of you well.
Sorry for being all blacked out
in your apartment. At least
I think there were two of you.

You see, Saturday night,
I was at Sugarland alone.
It was the night before
Valentine's Day (Saturday)
and I might have had a drink
or two too many.

I was hoping you could fill me in
on a few crucial details,
so I've put together a short list.
-Was I making out with one/
both of you at Sugarland?
-Did we meet outside?
-How did we decide to go back to your place?
-How long was I passed out on your couch
before I came too and left all scared?

Anyway, hope your week is going good
and I'm sorry for passing out at your place.
Since we're all living in BK and gay,
I figure even if I don't remember you
or what you look like (I don't),
you guys probably will recognize me,
so just tap me on the shoulder sometime
and we'll all have a good laugh about it.

And thanks again
for not killing/raping me.
Appreciate it.

DREAM GIRL IN THE REPUBLIC

You were dancing the Macarena
at Whisky Republic,
and I came up to chat with you.
You were wearing a sequined Holister crop top.
I had two polos on—both collars popped—
and a fresh-cut pair of jorts.

I bought you a rum and coke, extra lime.
We chatted a bit. You said
you were voting for Trump.
I showed you my Mitt Romney tattoo.
Despite our differences,
I think we both felt magic between us.

We ended up leaving the bar
and going to the Hot Club,
where we sang "I'm Blue" at karaoke.
You got mad because
I couldn't remember your name,
but I tried to convince you
that I couldn't remember mine either.

We shared a cigarette on the back deck.
You said you're trying to stop.
I said I'm trying to start.
I was so drunk that I fell onto the ground
and passed out for a good 60 seconds.

When a man tried to help me up,
I got really angry and embarrassed
and tried to fight the man.
You distracted me by flashing a nipple,
and I totally forgot
why I was angry in the first place.

We came back to my place,
and, on the way home,
I murdered an alley cat
to impress you.
When we got to my place,
I ordered pizza. I accidentally
dropped a slice on my hairy chest,
and you licked off all the sauce.

We watched Fox News
until the sun came up,
and then you left abruptly.
You said you remembered
something you had to do.
I never got your number.
I never even got your name.

And now I'm just awaking,
with crusty pizza sauce stains
on my chest hair.
And I'm wondering if you're out there.
Did I dream you?

PIZZA BOY

Oh pizza boy
you looked cute today.

Last time I saw you
I was drunk, we made out,
and then I kicked you out
of my apartment.

Sorry bout that.
I want a rematch

reply

MATT WHO VOTED FOR NIXON

I had a nice time with you
and I enjoyed the sex.
which is rare
due to my prudishness.

I am sorry I forgot
what you did
before you retired.
Was it boring?

Or, we should go
to the beach.
or you could peel yourself
away from the bar

and we could
go see a movie
about how rich people
hurt poor people
who are better than rich people.

OR!
we could do other stuff.

But not now.
Some other time.
I hope the glass doesnt kill you
Stop drinking!

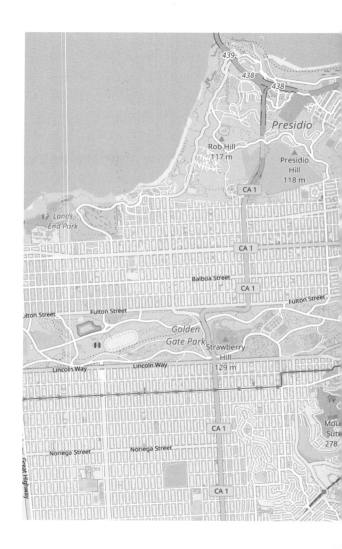

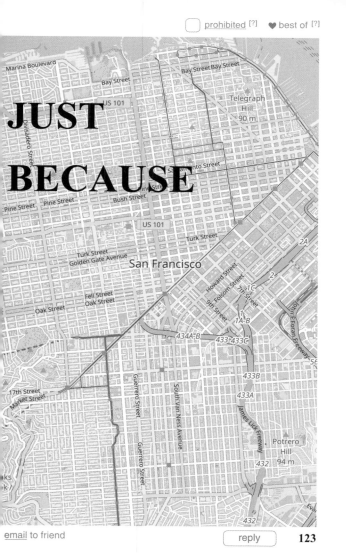

JUST BECAUSE

ORGANIC JERKY

What if
I went out west
and opened a shack
that had the best
organic, free range,
grass fed, artesian,
homemade beef jerky
in town

And I told jokes
and tap danced
while my dog cooked
the most unbelievable burgers
over hot coals
and we sold them
for only a buck

email to friend

reply

10 REASONS WE WON'T
BE HAVING A SECOND DATE

10. You answer the phone by saying "Hey, girl hey!!!"

9. The last book you read was an acting manual.

8. You check GRINDR while I'm close enough to see it happen.

7. You continually refer to Lady Gaga as a "ground breaking artist"

6. Deep V Neck.

5. The most fulfilling relationship you have is with your personal trainer.

4. The most fulfilling relationship you have is with your mother.

3. You're over 25 years old and still wearing Abercrombie and Fitch.

2. You have your own name tattooed on your body.

1. You don't drink.

That's just staggering.

THANKS FOR THE EDAMAME!

...and the napkin table shim.
and for that story
about the dead dog
in the duffel bag
with the unexpected conclusion.

just wanted to let you know
that you
are quite the gentleman.
hope you had a great rest of your evening!

sincerely,
girl in the leg cast
half king thursday night

p.s. no,
this is not
a hoax.

Q TRAIN--> INTO BROOKLYN:
BLACK T SHIRT, SHARP OBJECT

i was watching you
as you were busily undoing
a white piece of felt
from your canvas bag
with a sharp tool

i think the guy next to you was worried
and then i watched you read
and tried in vain to find out what book it was

you were tracing the sentences with your finger,
and mouthing the words
you had a ?beer? can in your bag,
wrapped in a paper bag.
i think it was open,
so it was probably empty

you didnt notice me—
and i liked that

you are tall and lean with shiny dark eyes
and messy hair
with what might have been a pencil
but looked like a piece of wood tucked into it
you also have nice ankles
brown leather shoes and no socks

you are incredibly fascinating
like a large, dirty, freight train elf
i made up stories

operator, operator

reply

TRICKY TJUSSE

We met at someone's birthday party
in Murray Hill last friday.
You and I were the ones
smoking cigarettes in the kitchen.
We shared a mutual appreciation
for Lawrence Lessig.

You gingerly wrote a name
on the back of my hand,
leading me to believe
I could use it
to find you on facebook…

and somehow you neglected
to mention the name was a fake!
Or rather, no such name
exists on facebook.
I was tricked!

I suppose I should have known
something was up after you
double checked the spelling.
I wonder if it was planned:
the way your roommate just happened
to mention missed connections
right before the two of you left?
A litmus test to gauge a guy's real intentions?
Or am I merely a pawn in your game,
and all you really wanted
was to have a poor sob write
a missed connection about you all along?

I should feel so used!
Tricky Tjusse, I like your style.

Alright, so now it's your turn:
maybe this email address
I've provided here is real...
and maybe it isn't!
I dare you to find out

YOU TOOK THE LAST SUNDAY TIMES

Dear check-shirted,
filthy-sandaled
paper grabber:
OK, the second to last Sunday Times.

You lunged for it while I didn't,
since I'm still trying to observe
some of the dignities of civilized life.

I had to take the last one,
the one that invariably
looks like it's been walked on
by an army.

I couldn't even read the front page
it was such a mess,
and I was too flustered to check it for all the
    sections––

when I got home
I discovered it had no book review.
This not only ruined my Sunday,
it has cast a pall over my entire week.

In the meantime, you probably
read only the sports section
and used the rest of the paper
to line your parrot cage.

You look like the kind of guy
who has one of those
muttering, clicking giant birds
with a stupid name like Otto
and a beak that can
punch a hole in an oil drum.

I hope he pecks a dent in your cortex
while he's sitting on your shoulder.
All the Justice That's Fit to Print

BULBS, OR, GIRL WITH HAIR AT SHOW

'Bulbs' is such a silly word
when you say it more than five times.
Were I to name each bulb,
I'd look to Greek mythology
and Saturday morning cartoons.
The bulbs were on the stage last night
at Pete's Candy Store.
Field Guides were under the low glow.

You: eyebrows like furry caterpillars,
asleep and dreaming above your eyes
of cocoons and future wings.
(and Jessica Tandy)

Me: a snaggletooth;
two diligent eyes (neither lazy);
hair growing (still at this age!)
in mostly conventional locales;
an evident yearning
to earn the approval of my peers;
an evident yearning
for furry and furless affections;
a coat evoking fields of nettles.
If I were a marine animal,
I'd be some sort of mollusk.

Bulbs bulbs bulbs bulbs bulbs...
Bulbs.

email to friend   reply

I NEVER CHEATED ON YOU

or you or you
or you or you
or you or you or you or you
or you or you
or you or you
or you or you or you

Published and distributed by Knock Knock
1635 Electric Ave.
Venice, CA 90291
knockknockstuff.com
Knock Knock is a registered trademark of Knock Knock LLC

Special thanks to craigslist and the *New York Times*, where several
of these poems first appeared.

ISBN: 978-168349022-7
UPC: 825703-50148-3

10 9 8 7 6 5 4 3 2 1